This Book is

Protected by
Instant IP

Engineering Land Value

The Proven Framework to Reduce Risk, Unlock Cash, and Maximize Returns

Carter Froelich

Other Books from Carter

*Land to Lots: How to Borrow Money You
Don't Have to Pay Back and LAUNCH
Master Planned Communities*

The *Land to Lots*™ Series
Fields to Fortune: Planning Your Bigger Future
Activating Your Fortune: Implementing Your Bigger Future
Counting Your Fortune: Managing Your Bigger Future

Engineering Land Value

THE PROVEN FRAMEWORK TO REDUCE RISK, UNLOCK CASH, AND MAXIMIZE RETURNS

CARTER FROELICH, CPA

Launch Development Finance Advisors
Launch-dfa.com
an affiliated company of
Land Advisors Organization
LandAdvisors.com

Printed in the United States of America
Published by Igniting Souls
PO Box 43, Powell, OH 43065
IgnitingSouls.com

LCCN: 2026900625
Paperback ISBN: 978-1-63680-618-1
Hardback ISBN: 978-1-63680-619-8
eBook ISBN: 978-1-63680-620-4

Available in paperback, hardcover, e-book, and audiobook.

Any Internet addresses (websites, blogs, etc.) and telephone numbers printed in this book are offered as a resource. They are not intended in any way to be or imply an endorsement by Igniting Souls, nor does Igniting Souls vouch for the content of these sites and numbers for the life of this book.

Some names and identifying details may have been changed to protect the privacy of individuals.

The publisher has not independently investigated or confirmed the accuracy of any such references and disclaims all responsibility for them. Nothing in this book should be construed as factual assertions about the character, conduct, or reputation of any individual or entity mentioned. Any resemblance to persons living or dead is purely coincidental unless explicitly stated.

The publisher expressly disclaims liability for any alleged loss, damage, or injury arising from any perceived defamatory content or reliance upon statements within this work. Responsibility for the views, depictions, and representations rests solely with the author.

All numerical examples, case studies, and financial illustrations in this book are for educational purposes only and do not represent actual projects or guaranteed outcomes.

Dedication

To the landowners, developers, and builders
who see possibility where others see only dirt.
To my colleagues at Launch and
Land Advisors Organization,
who share the mission of creating value
and building communities.
And to my family, who have tolerated my obsession
with real estate, development, and finance
for more years than any of us care to count.

—Carter

To Access Supplemental Documents
and Book Bonuses, Visit
EngineeringLandValue.com

Table of Contents

Note from Carter

I've been obsessed with the economics of land development for over forty years. It started, as many obsessions do, with a puzzle I couldn't solve.

Early in my career, I was working on a consulting engagement where two nearly identical parcels of land—same size, same general location, same basic development potential—were selling for wildly different prices. One was trading hands for millions more than the other. On paper, they looked the same. But someone was paying a significant premium for one of them, and I couldn't figure out why.

That mystery sent me down a rabbit hole that I've never really climbed out of. What I discovered was that the difference wasn't in the dirt; it was in what had been done to the dirt. One property had entitlements in place. It had development agreements with the jurisdiction. It had infrastructure financing mechanisms that would allow a builder to develop the land without crushing upfront capital requirements. The other parcel? It was raw, unentitled, and full of risk.

The premium buyer was paying for wasn't land. It was certainty. It was financing. It was reduced risk. It was a clear path from raw ground to finished lots to sold homes.

That realization changed the trajectory of my career. I became what I now call a "Land Residual Detective"—someone who looks at a piece of property and asks not, "What is this land worth?" but "What COULD this land be worth if we did everything right?"

This book is the distillation of over four decades of answering that question for landowners, developers, builders, and capital providers across the country. It's a practitioner's guide, not an academic treatise. I'm not going to burden you with theoretical frameworks or abstract concepts. Instead, I'm going to share the tools, strategies, and hard-won lessons that my team at Launch Development Finance Advisors (Launch) (Launch-dfa.com) uses every day to help our clients enhance and harvest land value.

At the heart of everything we do is a deceptively simple concept: land residual analysis. It's the lens through which we view every project, every deal, and every decision. If you understand how land residual value works—and more importantly, how to engineer it—you'll have a competitive advantage that most people in this business never develop.

This book is practical and story-driven because that's how I think. I've never been one for theory disconnected from application. Every concept in these pages has been tested in the real world, often through painful trial and error. The case studies are real (though I've changed some details to protect confidentiality). The strategies work. I know because we use them.

My goal is simple: I want you to finish this book with a working understanding of land residual analysis and a toolkit of strategies for increasing land value. Whether you're a landowner wondering how to get top dollar for your property, a developer looking to maximize returns, or a capital provider trying to underwrite risk more accurately, this book will help you make better decisions and avoid costly mistakes.

One more thing before we dive in. Throughout this book, you'll hear me talk about Launch and our strategic alignment with Land Advisors Organization. This isn't just marketing; it's central to how we serve our clients. Launch helps engineer land value through entitlements, infrastructure financing, and risk mitigation. Land Advisors helps harvest that value by connecting sellers with the right buyers at the right time. When you work with both of us, you get a seamless path from raw land to maximized returns.

So if you're holding a piece of land and wondering what it could become, or if you're looking at an acquisition and trying to figure out what it's really worth, I hope you'll reach out (carter@launch-dfa.com). But first, read this book. By the time you're done, you'll understand exactly why I'm so passionate about this work—and you'll have the knowledge to be a smarter, more effective participant in the land development game.

Let's get started.

—Carter Froelich, CPA
Managing Principal
Launch Development Finance Advisors

Introduction
THE LAND RESIDUAL DETECTIVE

Every development project is a puzzle. Think about it: you have a piece of land with certain physical characteristics, regulatory constraints, market conditions, infrastructure requirements, and financing needs. Your job as a developer—or as an advisor to developers—is to figure out how all these pieces fit together to create value.

I think of this puzzle-solving work as being a "Land Residual Detective." Like any good detective, we gather clues, test hypotheses, and ultimately arrive at an answer to the central question: What is this land currently worth, and how can we "engineer" it to be worth more?

THE PROJECT VISION

Every successful development starts with what we at Launch call The Project Vision™. This is the developer's picture of what the finished project will look like, who will buy it, and how the development will unfold over time. The Project Vision isn't just a dream; it's a detailed business plan that guides every decision from land acquisition through final lot/home sale.

Some developers plan to entitle a property and flip it to a builder. Others intend to take the project all the way through horizontal development, creating finished lots for sale. Still, others are vertical builders who will develop the lots, construct homes, and sell them to end users. Each of these business models requires a different Project Vision, and each has different implications for land value.

The key insight is this: even if you're planning to flip the land after entitlement, you need to think through the entire development process. Why? Because your buyer will. The value of entitled land depends on what a builder can do with it, and if you haven't thought through the downstream economics, you're leaving money on the table.

THE D.O.S.® FRAMEWORK: DANGERS, OPPORTUNITIES, STRENGTHS

Before we dive into the mechanics of land residual analysis, I want to introduce a diagnostic framework that we use at Launch to evaluate every project. It comes from Dan Sullivan and the Strategic Coach® organization, and it's called The D.O.S. Conversation®. (D.O.S. stands for Dangers, Opportunities, and Strengths.)

When we look at a potential project, we start by identifying the Dangers. What could go wrong? What are the regulatory hurdles? Where are the environmental risks? What are the infrastructure constraints? What market conditions could torpedo the deal?

Next, we look at Opportunities. What's special about this site? Are there infrastructure financing tools available that could reduce costs? Is the jurisdiction cooperative? Are there density bonuses or other entitlement strategies that could increase value?

Finally, we assess Strengths. What does the developer bring to the table? Experience? Relationships? Capital? A track record with this jurisdiction?

The D.O.S. framework gives us a structured way to think about the factors that will ultimately show up in our land residual analysis. A project with significant Dangers will require careful thought to reduce and/or eliminate these Dangers; otherwise, land value will be impaired. A project with strong Opportunities may allow us to engineer additional value. And a developer with real Strengths may be able to execute a business plan that others couldn't.

A BIT ABOUT MY BACKGROUND

Since I'll be your guide through the world of land residual analysis, you should probably know a little about who I am and why I think I'm qualified to write this book.

I'm Carter Froelich, a CPA, and the Managing Principal of Launch Development Finance Advisors. I've been working in real estate finance and consulting for over four decades, which means I've seen multiple market cycles, countless deals (both successful and not), and more spreadsheets than any human being should have to look at.

I'm a licensed real estate advisor with Land Advisors Organization, the nation's largest land brokerage firm focused exclusively on land. I'm also a former Arizona State Certified Real Estate Appraiser, though I should confess that I lost that license not through any professional misconduct but because I forgot to notify the Arizona Board of Appraisal when I moved offices. (They're very particular about address changes, it turns out. Who knew?) My appraisal background, however, gave me a deep grounding in valuation methodology that informs everything I do today.

Launch is a transaction-based real estate consulting firm that works exclusively on behalf of the private sector—we have no mixed loyalties. What does that mean? It means we don't just produce reports and collect fees; we help our clients get deals done. We're in the trenches with landowners, developers, and builders, working to finance infrastructure, reduce costs, mitigate risk, and enhance project profitability and returns. Our mission is to be the hero to the development community, and we take that mission seriously.

THE LAUNCH SEQUENCE®

Over the years, I've developed a systematic approach to finance project infrastructure, reduce project costs, and mitigate project risks, which we call The Launch Sequence®. It's a step-by-step process for identifying value-creation opportunities and implementing strategies to capture that value.

I've written extensively about The Launch Sequence in my *Bigger Future Land to Lots* trilogy (which you can find on), and I won't repeat all of that material here. What I want you to understand for purposes of this book is that every strategy in The Launch Sequence, every entitlement tool, every financing mechanism, every risk mitigation technique ultimately shows up in one place: the land residual analysis.

The land residual analysis is the scorecard. It's how we measure whether our strategies are working. When we negotiate a Development Agreement (DA) that locks in favorable terms, the benefit shows up as an increase in land residual value. When we create a special district that allows us to finance infrastructure with bonds instead of cash, the benefit shows up as increased land residual value. When we reduce risk through the Pre-annexation and Development Agreement (PADA), DA, reimbursement agreement, and/or cost-sharing agreement, the benefit shows up as increased land residual value.

MAKING VALUE "REAL"

Here's a crucial concept that many people miss: it's not enough to have strategies that could increase land value. The strategies must be memorialized in binding agreements to become real and bankable.

Think about it from a buyer's perspective. If a seller tells you, "The city has verbally agreed to let us form a community facilities district (CFD)," how much would you pay for that? Not much, because a verbal agreement is not enforceable. But if the seller can show you a signed and recorded PADA with specific CFD bond authorization, property tax rate caps, and governance provisions, you have something you can take to the bank—literally.

Throughout this book, I'll emphasize the importance of documentation. Entitlement agreements. DAs. District formation documents. reimbursement agreements (collectively, the Agreement(s)). These aren't just legal paper-work; they're the foundation of supportable land valuation. Without them, you have potential. With them, you have "engineered" value.

Launch Tip

Value isn't real until it's documented. Before you claim credit for "engineering" additional land value, ask yourself: Is this benefit memorialized in a binding Agreement that will transfer to my buyer?

With that foundation laid, let's dive into the mechanics of land residual analysis. In the next chapter, we'll answer the fundamental question: What exactly is land residual value, and why does it matter?

INTRODUCING CHAPTER LAND VALUE PLAYBOOKS

Engineering Land Value explains the concepts, frameworks, and strategies for using land residual analysis to finance infrastructure, reduce costs, and mitigate risks with the goal of maximizing project returns and enhancing land residual value.

The Chapter Land Value Playbooks ("Playbooks") are the action layer that sits on top of that framework. They are designed to:

- Turn ideas into repeatable habits and checklists.

- Help you apply each chapter's concepts to your actual deals.

- Give you and your team simple prompts you can run through in a few minutes, but that will materially improve the quality of your decisions over time.

HOW TO USE THE PLAYBOOKS

1. Read **Engineering Land Value**, chapter-by-chapter. The main text provides you with the why" and "how" through detailed examples, case studies, and context.

2. After each chapter, review the corresponding Playbook section. For example, after reading Chapter 2, "What Is Land Residual Value?", work through the Chapter 2 Playbook: Making the Residual Real.

3. Treat the Quick Actions as checklists, not suggestions.

   The value comes from repetition.

   For each chapter:

   - Pick at least one Quick Action and apply it immediately to a live or recent project transaction.

   - Over time, work toward making all of them part of your standard underwriting and negotiation process

4. Use the Playbooks with your team. The Playbooks are ideal for:

- Land committee and investment committee discussions

- Weekly acquisition or entitlement meetings

- Training junior team members on how you want work done

5. Revisit the Playbooks at each stage of The Launch Sequence. Different actions matter at different points:

- At Vision (Stage 1), focus on residual basics, drivers of value, and your Project Vision®.

- At Assessment Development (Stage 2), focus on your Project DOS™ issues and scenario testing.

- At Strategy and Execution (Stages 3–4), focus on financing, special districts, development and reimbursement agreements, as well as cost control.

- At Value Harvest (Stage 5), focus on memorialization and presentation of the Engineered Value.

Use this document as a working manual. Mark it up. Add your own notes, templates, and internal standards. Over time, you'll have a customized operating system for how you and your team underwrite, negotiate, and engineer land value.

What Is Land Residual Value?

Let's start with a simple definition. Land residual value is the maximum price a developer or home builder can pay for land while still achieving their required return metrics.

Read that again because it's important.

We're not talking about what land is "worth" in some abstract sense. We're talking about what a specific developer or home builder with a specific business plan can afford to pay for a specific piece of land while still making the project financially viable.

This distinction matters because it shifts our focus from the land itself to the development opportunity the land represents. A vacant parcel isn't just dirt; it's a bundle of rights and possibilities. And the value of those rights and possibilities depends on what you plan to do with them.

THE RESIDUAL LAND VALUE FORMULA

The basic formula for estimating residual land value is elegantly simple:

$$\textit{Residual Land Value} =$$
$$\textit{Gross Development Value} - (\textit{Construction Costs} +$$
$$\textit{Fees} + \textit{Financing} + \textit{Developer Profit})$$

Let me break this down piece by piece.

Gross Development Value (GDV) is the total revenue you expect to generate from the completed project. For a residential home builder development, this is the sum of all home sales. For a developer's single-family lot development, it's the sum of all lot sales to builders. GDV represents the "top line"—the estimated maximum revenue the project can generate.

From GDV, we subtract all the **costs required to develop the project**: construction costs, professional fees, permitting costs, financing costs, marketing expenses, and so on. We also subtract developer profit—the average return the developer/builder requires to take on the risk of the project.

What's left over—the **Residual Land Value**—is what the developer/builder can afford to pay for the land.

UNDERSTANDING GROSS DEVELOPMENT VALUE

Gross Development Value deserves some additional explanation because it's the starting point for everything else. GDV is forward-looking. It's an estimate of what the project will generate in the future, based on current market conditions and reasonable projections.

For residential developments, GDV typically comes from analyzing comparable sales in the market, adjusted for the specific characteristics of your project. What are similar homes selling for? What premiums do buyers pay for views, lot size, or proximity to amenities? What's the likely absorption rate—how quickly will homes sell? What is the ratio of finished lot sales price to home price?

This is where market research becomes critical. A land residual analysis is only as good as its assumptions, and the GDV assumption is arguably the most important one. Get it wrong, and everything else falls apart. This is why, when presenting your assumptions to a land committee or a potential buyer, it is critical to provide a well-documented recent third-party market study or comparable lot and/or home sales comparables.

COMPARISON WITH OTHER VALUATION METHODS

The residual approach isn't the only way to value land. Let me briefly describe two other common methods and explain why the residual approach is often superior for development land.

SALES COMPARISON APPROACH

The sales comparison approach values land by comparing recent sales of similar properties. You find comparable sales, adjust for differences, and arrive at a value estimate.

This approach works well for commodity properties—land that's essentially interchangeable with other parcels in the area. But development land is rarely a commodity. The value of a development site depends heavily on what can be built there, the entitlements in place, the available infrastructure, and a host of other factors that vary enormously from site to site.

The sales comparison approach also looks backward. It tells you what buyers have paid in the past, not what a developer can afford to pay today for a specific project.

INCOME CAPITALIZATION APPROACH

The income capitalization approach values property based on the income it generates. Typically, you estimate net operating income and divide by a capitalization rate to arrive at value.

This approach is ideal for income-producing properties, such as apartment buildings or shopping centers. But raw development land typically doesn't generate recurring dependable "rental" income; it generates costs (property taxes, maintenance, carrying costs) until it's developed and then begins to generate lumpy revenue events over time through the sale of super-pads, finished lots, and special district bond issuances. The standard income approach to value simply doesn't fit the development context.

RESIDUAL IS SUPERIOR FOR DEVELOPMENT LAND

The residual approach is forward-looking and development-specific. It asks the right question: Given what I plan to build and sell, what can I afford to pay for this land?

More importantly, the residual approach reveals the drivers of value. If you understand the formula, you can see exactly how changes in GDV, costs, or required profit affect the bottom line. ***This makes the residual approach not just a valuation tool but a strategic planning and value engineering tool.***

THE KEY INSIGHT: YOU CAN MOVE THE LEVERS

Here's the most important concept in this entire book: ***Once you understand the components of residual land value, you can consciously work to move them in your favor.***

Want to increase land value? You have a few basic options:

- Increase GDV (more revenue)

- Decrease development costs (lower costs)

- Defer development costs (cash outflows later)

- Accelerate cash into the project cash flow (cash receipts sooner)

- Reduce the required profit (by reducing risk)

Every strategy in this book, every entitlement technique, every financing tool, every risk mitigation approach, works by moving one or more of these levers. The land residual analysis is how we measure the impact.

A Note on Builder Profit Versus Developer Profit

In practice, it is critical to distinguish between builder profit and developer (entrepreneurial) profit when preparing a land residual analysis.

Builder profit should always be treated as a cost of production, either embedded in vertical construction costs if you are building homes, or implicitly in the lot prices you assume if you are selling finished lots to builders. This is done because it represents the market price of construction services.

Developer profit, by contrast, is the entrepreneurial reward for assembling land, securing entitlements, arranging financing, and managing risk, and it should be modeled either as an explicit margin (for example, a target percentage of total development cost or of gross development value in a simple residual) or implicitly through the discount rate or IRR hurdle in a discounted cash flow residual, but not both at the same time. If you include a separate "developer profit" line and also apply a discount rate that reflects that same required return, you will double-count the profit requirement and understate the land residual.

A SIMPLE ILLUSTRATIVE EXAMPLE

Let me show you how this works with a simple example. We'll use round numbers to make the math easy—this is for illustration only, not a representation of any actual project. The example below is a "quick and dirty" assessment that a land developer may use to check a potential land development opportunity. *The table below is shown for illustrative purposes only. If you want a true, risk-aware land residual analysis, the analysis should be anchored in home builder economics, even if you plan on selling land or lots.*

Exhibit 2.1 – Simple Land Residual Calculation (Illustrative Example)

Description	Amount
Gross Development Value (200 lots × $80,000/lot)	$16,000,000
Less: Construction Costs	($8,000,000)
Less: Professional Fees	($800,000)
Less: Permitting & Impact Fees	($1,200,000)
Less: Financing Costs	($1,000,000)
Less: Marketing & Sales	($500,000)
Less: Developer Profit (15% of costs)	($1,725,000)
Estimated Residual Land Value	**$2,775,000**
Per Acre (100 acres)	$27,750
Per Lot (200 lots)	$13,875

In this simple example, the developer can afford to pay up to $2,775,000 for the land—about $27,750 per acre or $13,875 per finished lot—while still achieving their required 15 percent profit margin.

Now here's where it gets interesting. What if we could increase the lot prices by 10 percent? Or reduce construction costs by 5 percent? Or use a special district to shift some of the infrastructure costs off the developer's balance sheet? Each of these changes would flow directly through to increased residual land value.

We'll explore exactly how to make those improvements in the chapters that follow.

Launch Tip – Don't Confuse Seller's Ask with Land Value

A common mistake is accepting the seller's asking price as "land value." The asking price is just a number someone wrote down. True land value is what a developer can afford to pay while still making their required return. These numbers may be very different, and the gap between them often determines whether a project gets done.

NOTE: The single-column analysis above has one significant limitation: it doesn't account for timing. In reality, costs and revenues occur over time. Interest accrues. Money has time value. A dollar received three years from now is worth less than a dollar today.

More sophisticated analyses incorporate timing through discounted cash flow (DCF) models. These models project costs and revenues by period (usually monthly or quarterly) and discount future cash flows to present value.

For now, understand that the simple single-column static model is a useful starting point, but for significant investments, you'll want to develop or commission a timing-aware DCF analysis. We'll discuss this more in later chapters

CHAPTER 2 ACTION PLAYBOOK: MAKING THE RESIDUAL REAL

The concepts in Chapter 2 ("What Is Land Residual Value?") are only valuable if you start using them immediately. Use the following prompts to turn "residual value" from a concept into a working discipline in your business.

Quick Actions You Can Take Now

1. *Reverse-engineer your last three land transactions.* Pull your last three land transactions and do a rough residual calculation for each. Compare what you

actually paid to what the residual land value would suggest based on realistic revenue, cost, and profit assumptions.

2. *Write down your current rule of thumb for developer profit.*
   Is it 15 percent on cost? 10 percent on revenue? What is your target IRR? Is the target rate inclusive or exclusive of developer profit? Could you be double-counting developer profit and thereby missing out on deals because you are offering too little? Whatever your profit margins are and how you are using them in your analysis, get them out of your head and onto paper. Check your assumptions and, going forward, treat it as a deliberate, thoughtful input, not whatever is "left over."

3. *Pick one upcoming project opportunity and commit to a residual analysis before you sign.*
   Identify the next land opportunity you're seriously considering. Even if it's a simple spreadsheet, run a residual analysis before you make an offer or sign a PSA.

4. *Build a one-page land residual spreadsheet template.*
   Create a simple one-page template with:

   - GDV at the top

   - Major cost buckets (direct, hard, soft, fees, financing, sales/marketing)

- Explicit developer/builder profit requirement

- Residual land value at the bottom (total, per acre, per lot)

Why Use the Land Residual Method?

Now that you understand what land residual value is, let me explain why it's the most powerful valuation tool for land development. The advantages are numerous and stem from the method's fundamental focus on the home builder's perspective.

KEY ADVANTAGES OF THE RESIDUAL METHOD

DEVELOPER-FOCUSED

The residual method answers the question developers and builders actually need answered: "What can I afford to pay?" Other valuation methods might tell you what similar land has sold for or what a property might be worth in theory. The residual method tells you what makes financial sense for your specific deal.

COMPREHENSIVE

The residual method forces you to think through every cost category: construction, fees, financing, profit. There's no hiding from uncomfortable numbers. If your impact fees are going to eat up $3 million, that shows up in the analysis. If your construction costs are higher than industry averages, that shows up too. The method is brutally honest, which is exactly what you need when you're committing millions of dollars to a project.

FLEXIBLE AND ADAPTABLE

Unlike static valuation methods, the residual approach can easily accommodate different development scenarios. What if home prices are lower than expected? What if you sell homes faster than expected? What if you can negotiate lower impact fees? What if interest rates rise? You can model all of these scenarios and see exactly how they affect your bottom line.

DECISION-READY

The output of a residual analysis isn't just a number - it's a decision-making tool. If your residual value is higher than the asking price, you have a potential deal. If it's lower, you know you need to either negotiate a better price or find ways to improve the project economics. The analysis directly supports action.

RISK-AWARE

By requiring you to specify your target profit margin or discount rate, the residual method builds risk assessment into the valuation process. A riskier project requires a higher return margin, which reduces the residual value. This automatically adjusts the land value for risk - something other methods often ignore.

ENHANCES STAKEHOLDER AND LENDER CONFIDENCE

When you present a project to the land committee, investors, lenders, or buyers, a well-constructed residual analysis demonstrates that you've done your homework. You've thought through the revenue projections, cost estimates, financing structure, and return requirements. This level of analysis builds confidence and makes it easier to negotiate a transaction.

REFLECTS DEVELOPMENT-SPECIFIC FACTORS

Every development site is unique. The residual method captures that uniqueness by incorporating site-specific costs, entitlements, and revenue projections. Two adjacent parcels might have vastly different residual values based on their specific development constraints and opportunities.

Exhibit 3.1 – Key Advantages of the Land Residual Method

Advantage	Description
Developer-Focused	Answers the question developers need answered: What can I afford to pay?
Comprehensive	Forces consideration of all cost categories with no place to hide
Flexible	Easily accommodates different scenarios and assumptions
Decision-Ready	Output directly supports go/no-go decisions
Risk-Aware	Target profit margin builds risk assessment into valuation
Builds Confidence	Demonstrates thorough analysis to land committees, investors, lenders and/or buyers.
Site-Specific	Captures unique characteristics of each development opportunity

CASE STUDY: FOOTHILL RANCH, CORONA, CALIFORNIA

Let me tell you a story that illustrates why the residual method is so powerful when combined with proper preparation and documentation. While some of my examples may be older in nature, I encourage you only to focus on the concepts, as they not only worked in the past, but they work in the present as well.

Early in my career, I was working at Kenneth Leventhal & Company (KL) in Newport Beach, California. KL was the premier real estate consulting firm in the country at the time (and was later sold to Ernst & Young in the mid 1990's), and we worked on significant transactions.

A partnership came to us with a challenge. They owned a large property—mostly orchards—in the Foothill Ranch area near Corona. They wanted to maximize the value of the land, but they knew that selling raw, unentitled acreage would leave money on the table.

Here's what we did:

- Hired a seasoned project manager from the Irvine Company to oversee the entitlement process

- Planned and entitled the property for residential development, working through all the jurisdictional requirements

- Prepared detailed cost estimates using engineers and other consultants

- Created a CFD to provide a mechanism for financing public infrastructure

- Conducted comprehensive market feasibility analysis, including pricing studies, absorption projections, and premium analysis for views and other amenities

- Prepared a detailed land residual analysis incorporating all of the above assumptions, including the CFD terms

- Provided the complete, fully functioning residual land model in Lotus 1-2-3 (I'm dating myself) and all supporting assumptions to every bidder, so they could understand exactly what they were buying

- Assembled a "war room" of documents—every study, every Agreement, every piece of analysis—for buyer due diligence

- Advertised the opportunity to all KL clients, which included the nation's largest land developers and homebuilders

- Took sealed bids and negotiated the final sale

The result? The property sold for approximately 20 percent more than the partnership had originally expected.

Why did we achieve such a premium? Because we had done everything. The entitlements were in place. The CFD was formed. The cost estimates were detailed and credible. The market analysis was thorough. And critically, all of this was documented, Agreements recorded, and available for buyer review.

Buyers were willing to pay more because we had eliminated uncertainty and transaction risk. They weren't buying potential—they were buying a defined opportunity with known costs and quantified risks. The residual analysis wasn't just a valuation tool; it became a sales tool.

Case in Point: Foothill Ranch

- *Raw orchards transformed into entitled residential land*

- *Complete entitlements, CFD formation, and detailed cost estimates*

- *Full documentation available to all bidders*

- *Result: ~20 percent premium over expected value*

- *Key lesson: When everything is done and documented, value is real and defensible*

Developer Beware:
The Cost of Skipping the Homework

Some sellers try to sell on potential: "This land COULD be entitled for 500 units." Smart buyers discount that potential heavily because they know the risks. Entitlement battles, environmental challenges, community opposition—all of these can derail a project. If you want top dollar, do the work. Entitled land with documented infrastructure financing is worth far more than raw land with possibilities.

The Foothill Ranch experience taught me a lesson I've never forgotten: ***The land residual analysis isn't just about estimating value. It's about understanding all the factors that drive value, documenting them thoroughly, and presenting them in a way that gives buyers confidence.***

In the chapters that follow, we'll dive deeper into the mechanics of the residual method and explore the specific strategies you can use to engineer higher land values. But

I want you to keep the Foothill Ranch story in mind as a north star: this is what we're aiming for. Complete analysis, thorough documentation, and maximum value realization.

CHAPTER 3 PLAYBOOK: MOVING BEYOND COMPARABLES

Chapter 3 ("Why Use the Land Residual Method?") makes the case for moving beyond comparable sales as your primary valuation tool. Use these prompts to shift from a comps-only mindset to a land residual-based discipline.

Quick Actions You Can Take Now

1. *Perform a Land Value Diagnostic on how you currently decide what to pay for land.*
   List the top three ways you make pricing decisions today (e.g., $/acre comps, broker opinion of value, "what the seller wants"). For each, ask:

Is this forward-looking (based on what will be built) or backward-looking (based on what sold yesterday)? Which do you think is more credible and why?

2. *Revisit your last land purchase or sale.*
   If you had run a residual analysis at the time:

   - How might it have changed your view of the asking price?

- Would you have structured the transaction differently (options, takedowns, contingencies, land banker, seller financing, JV, etc.)?

3. *On the next purchase or offering, do your own land residual analysis before reviewing the document.* When a new package crosses your desk, draft your own rough residual estimate **before** you focus on the seller's price or your asking price. Treat the seller's number as a negotiating data point, not a starting truth. Conversely, how will potential buyers of your property review your land package and supporting land residual analysis?

How the Method Works—Step by Step

Now we get into the mechanics. The land residual analysis is a mathematical model, and like all models, it's built on assumptions. Before we dive into the steps, let me offer a few words of caution and wisdom.

A WORD ABOUT ASSUMPTIONS

I'm reminded of Sergeant Joe Friday from the old *Dragnet* television series: "Just the facts, ma'am." ***When building a residual analysis, you want facts: real data, verified numbers, credible projections. Assumptions should be grounded in reality, not wishful or aspirational thinking.***

The legendary real estate investor Sam Zell once said, "I don't make assumptions." What he meant was that he doesn't accept assumptions uncritically. He digs into the data, questions the projections, and tests the premises. That's the mindset you need when building a residual analysis.

At the same time, don't get wrapped around the axle trying to achieve perfection. You'll never have perfect information. The goal is reasoned, supportable assumptions - numbers you can defend with data and logic. If someone asks why you assumed a 3 percent annual price apprecia-tion, you should have an answer based on market research, not hope.

STEP 1: ESTIMATE GROSS DEVELOPMENT VALUE

The first step is estimating the value of your completed project. For residential developments, this typically means projecting home sale prices and absorption rates.

MARKET COMPARABLES

Start with comparable sales in the market. What are similar homes selling for? What price per square foot are buyers paying? What premiums do they pay for views, lot size, or upgraded finishes? What are the lot-to-home price ratios in the market?

Be careful with comparables. Not all sales are truly com-parable. A home in an established neighborhood with ma-ture landscaping and proven schools isn't the same as a new home in an untested community. Adjust for differ-ences and be conservative in your adjustments.

EXPERT APPRAISALS AND MARKET STUDIES

For significant projects, consider commissioning third-party market studies or appraisals. Firms like RCLCO, John Burns Real Estate Consulting, Zonda, the Concord Group, and Clarity specialize in this type of work. Their independent analysis adds credibility to your assumptions and may uncover market dynamics you've missed.

PRICE PER UNIT AND PREMIUMS

Think carefully about your product mix and pricing strategy. Different lot sizes command different prices. View lots typically sell for premiums. Lots backing a commercial facility may sell for a discount. Premium locations within the project (near amenities, away from traffic) affect pricing.

Build these nuances into your GDV projection. A sophisticated analysis might have dozens of different lot types, each with its own price assumption.

STEP 2: IDENTIFY AND SUM ALL DEVELOPMENT COSTS

Next, you need to identify every cost required to take the project from raw land to completed lots or homes. This is where the discipline of the residual method really pays off—it forces you to think through everything.

CONSTRUCTION COSTS

This includes all physical construction: grading, utilities, streets, drainage, landscaping, and (for vertical development) direct and indirect home construction costs as well as related overhead. Get detailed cost estimates from engineers and contractors. Get the recent Opinion of Probable Costs (OPC) from your civil engineer, or better yet, recent actual bids based upon approved plans (the best cost data).

Don't forget site-specific challenges. Difficult topography, rock excavation, drainage, environmental remediation, and utility extensions can add significantly to costs.

PROFESSIONAL FEES

Budget for all the professionals you'll need: civil engineers, land planners, architects, environmental consultants, legal counsel, entitlement consultants, and so on. These fees can add up quickly on complex projects.

PERMITTING AND REGULATORY COSTS

This is a big one. Development impact fees (DIFs), utility connection fees, park fees, school fees, traffic mitigation fees—the list goes on (especially in states like California). Some jurisdictions have fee schedules published online. Others require negotiation. In either case, get hard numbers.

Don't forget permit fees, plan check fees, and inspection fees. They're usually smaller than impact fees, but they add up quickly.

FINANCING COSTS

Unless you're paying cash for everything (rare), you'll have financing costs. Budget for loan origination fees (points), interest during construction, and any required reserves. The financing structure significantly impacts total costs.

MARKETING AND SALES

You need to sell your lots or homes. Budget for real estate commissions, marketing materials, model homes (for vertical builders), signage, and ongoing sales overhead.

AGENCY MITIGATION AND SUBSIDIES

Some jurisdictions require developer contributions for projects such as fire stations, community centers, or affordable housing. These "mitigation" costs need to be included in your analysis.

CONTINGENCY

Things go wrong. Costs overrun. Surprises happen. A prudent analysis includes contingency allowances—typically 5 percent to 10 percent of hard costs, depending on the project's risk profile.

BUILDER PROFIT

Finally, you need to include builder profit. This is the return required to compensate for the risk and capital invested in the project. Profit margins typically range from 8 percent to 15 percent of costs or GDV, depending on risk level and market conditions.

Note that builder profit isn't "extra"; it's a real cost of development. Without adequate profit, no rational developer would take on the risk.

Launch Tip: Build Your Assumptions Library

Over time, build a library of cost assumptions you can use as starting points for new projects. What do impact fees typically run in different jurisdictions? What are the current construction costs per linear foot of standard arterial, collector, and local street widths? What are typical soft cost percentages? Having a library of benchmarks helps you quickly sanity-check new analyses.

STEP 3: ESTIMATE RESIDUAL LAND VALUE

Once you have GDV and total costs, the math is simple: subtract costs from GDV to get residual land value.

**Residual Land Value =
GDV – Total Costs (including profit)**

Express your result in total dollars, dollars per acre, and dollars per lot (or per unit). These different metrics are useful for different purposes—comparing land prices (per acre), analyzing lot economics (per lot), and negotiating total purchase prices (total dollars).

THE LIMITATION OF SIMPLE SINGLE-COLUMN ANALYSIS

The simple approach I've described so far has one significant limitation: it doesn't account for timing. In reality, costs and revenues occur over time. Interest accrues.

Money has time value. A dollar received three years from now is worth less than a dollar today.

More sophisticated analyses incorporate timing through discounted cash flow (DCF) models. These models project costs and revenues by period (usually monthly or quarterly) and discount future cash flows to present value.

For now, understand that the simple static model is a useful starting point, but for significant investments, you'll want to develop or commission a timing-aware DCF analysis. We'll discuss this more in later chapters.

ILLUSTRATIVE EXAMPLE: DETAILED PRO FORMA

Let's look at a more detailed example. Remember, these numbers are illustrative only; they don't represent any actual project.

***Exhibit 4.1 – Detailed Land Residual Pro Forma
(Illustrative Example)***

Description	Assumption	Amount
Revenue		
Home Sales	350 Homes / $550,000/Home	$192,500,000
Options/Upgrades	$23,000/Home	$17,250,000
Total Revenue		**$209,750,000**
Costs		
Home Construction Costs		
Direct Home Construction Costs	Avg. Home SF 2,225SF @ $63/PSF	$49,061,250
Options/Upgrades Costs	$15,200/Home	$5,320,000
Building Permit	$5,600/Home	$1,960,000
Soft & Financing Costs	15%	$31,462,500
Builder Profit Margin	8% (Gross Revenue)	$16,780,000
Total Home Costs		**$104,583,750**
Finished Lot Value	Gross Revenue - Home Costs	$105,166,250
Finished Lot Value / Per Lot	**350 Lots**	**$300,475**
Site Improvements		
Backbone Infrastructure	$25,500 / Lot	$12,425,000
In-Tract Improvements	$95,350 / Lot	$33,372,500
Impact Fees	$25,400 / Lot	$19,050,000
Consultants	$5,500 / Lot	$4,125,000
Total Site Improvements		**$68,972,500**
Estimated Paper Lot Value	Finished Lot Value - Site Improvement Costs	$36,193,750
Estimated Paper Lot Value / Lot		**$48,258**
Land Residual Per Acre	**200 Acres**	**$180,969**

In this example, the developer can afford to pay up to $36.2 million for the land—roughly $181,00 per acre, or $48,300 per paper lot—while achieving their 8 percent profit target.

Notice how each line item in the analysis can be examined and potentially improved. Can we reduce impact fees through negotiation or a special district? Can we improve lot prices through better amenities or positioning? Can we reduce construction costs through value engineering and/or a special district? Each improvement flows directly to the bottom line and, as a result, residual land value.

Developer Beware:
The Dangers of Wishful Thinking in Pro Forma

I've seen too many deals go bad because someone built a pro forma full of aggressive assumptions. Above-market prices. Below-market costs. Aggressive absorption. Minimal contingency. On paper, the project looked great. In reality, it was a disaster waiting to happen.

Build conservative assumptions. Use real market data. Include adequate contingency. If the project doesn't work with conservative numbers, don't convince yourself it will work by tweaking the spreadsheet. The spreadsheet doesn't care; reality does.

CHAPTER 4 ACTION PLAYBOOK: BUILDING YOUR RESIDUAL MUSCLE

Chapter 4 ("How the Method Works—Step by Step") lays out the mechanics. The next step is to make them part of your standard underwriting and/or offering process.

QUICK ACTIONS YOU CAN TAKE NOW

1. *Create a residual land value spreadsheet template.* In Excel (or your preferred spreadsheet tool), build a basic model with:

   - **Inputs Tab:** unit counts, prices, key cost assump-tions, profit requirement

- **Discounted Cash Flow (DCF):** Create your residual land value DCF model to allow for the projection of cash flows and the "discounting" of the cash flows to today's present value using the required IRR

- **Summary Tab:** GDV, total costs (by category), profit, residual (total / per acre / per lot)

2. *Run three cost scenarios on your next evaluation.* For your next deal, estimate costs in three cases

   - Optimistic

   - Base

   - Conservative

Note how sensitive the residual land value is to each scenario. This will tell you where to focus your diligence.

3. *Research fees in at least one key jurisdiction.* For a city or county where you're active:

   - Pull the latest impact fee and utility connection fee schedules.

   - Confirm how and when fees are collected (plat, permit, CO).

   - Note any published special district, credit, or reimbursement policies.

4. *Make your profit requirement explicit.*
   Write down your minimum acceptable:

- Profit on cost **or**

- Profit on revenue **or**

- Target project-level IRREquity Multiple

Use this consistently across deals instead of backing into it after the fact.

What Impacts Land Residual Value?

Now that you understand how to estimate land residual value, let's explore what drives it. Understanding these drivers is the key to engineering higher values.

I organize the drivers of land residual value into three primary categories: Cash Flow, Velocity, and Discount Rate. Everything else is a derivative of these three.

THE THREE PRIMARY DRIVERS

CASH FLOW: MORE IN, LESS OUT

The first driver is straightforward: cash flow. You want more revenue and less cost.

On the revenue side, this means higher sale prices, better product mix, faster sales, and premium positioning. Can you achieve price premiums for views, lot size, or location? Can you add amenities that buyers will pay for and accelerate the sale pace? Can you position the project in a way that commands above-market pricing and/or sales velocity?

On the cost side, this means efficient design, smart phasing, special districts, negotiated fees, and rigorous cost control. Can you reduce impact fees for developer/builder and/or special district-constructed public improvements, or negotiate them? Can you phase infrastructure to minimize initial capital outflows and carrying costs? Can you value-engineer the design without sacrificing lots and/or marketable quality?

VELOCITY: FASTER IS BETTER

The second driver is velocity: the timing of cash flows. Revenue sooner is better than revenue later. Costs later are better than costs sooner.

This is the time value of money at work. A dollar received today can be invested and earn returns. A dollar received five years from now cannot. Similarly, a cost incurred today requires financing; a cost deferred reduces carrying costs.

Velocity improvements show up most clearly in DCF analyses, but they matter even in simple models. Faster absorption means faster revenue, lower carrying costs, and reduced risk. This is something we at Launch are always striving to accelerate, and it allows us to create the MUD , which has forever changed the way residential communities are financed in Texas.

DISCOUNT RATE: LESS RISK, MORE VALUE

The third driver is the discount rate used to value future cash flows. Lower discount rates mean higher present values.

The discount rate has two components: the risk-free rate (what you could earn on a zero-risk investment) and a risk premium (the extra return required for taking development risk). You can't control the risk-free rate; that's set by market conditions. But you can reduce the risk premium by de-risking the project.

Every risk mitigation strategy—entitlements, DAs, pre-approved financing structures—reduces the risk premium investors require. This flows directly to higher land value.

Exhibit 5.1 – Primary Drivers of Land Residual Value

Advantage	Description	Effect on Residual Value
Cash Flow – Revenue	Higher prices, premiums, better product mix	Increases GDV → Higher residual
Cash Flow – Costs	Lower construction, reduced fees, efficient design	Decreases costs → Higher residual
Velocity – Revenue	Faster absorption, earlier lot releases	Earlier revenue → Higher present value
Velocity – Costs	Deferred spending, phased infrastructure	Lower carrying costs → Higher residual
Discount Rate	Reduced risk through entitlements, agreements	Lower required returns → Higher present value

THE BIG FACTORS: WHAT REALLY MOVES THE NEEDLE

Within this framework, certain factors have outsized impacts on land residual value. Let me highlight the most important ones.

HIGHER PROJECTED SALE PRICES

Price is a powerful lever. A 5 percent increase in sale prices flows almost entirely to the bottom line (costs don't change much with price). For a project with $20 million in GDV, a 5 percent price improvement is equivalent to $1 million in additional value.

Price premiums can come from many sources: superior product design, better amenities, preferred school districts, views, larger lots, or simply better marketing and positioning. The key is understanding what buyers value and designing the project to deliver it.

IMPROVED LOCATION CHARACTERISTICS

Some location advantages are given by nature—you can't move a mountain or create a lake. But you can choose sites wisely and maximize the value of natural amenities through thoughtful planning.

Proximity to existing infrastructure is a huge factor. A site adjacent to existing utilities, roads, and services has lower development costs than a site that requires running miles of backbone infrastructure to kick off services. These cost savings flow directly to residual value.

Adjacency to good school districts, employment centers, and retail/commercial amenities also supports higher prices. Buyers pay premiums for convenience and quality of life.

Case in Point: When a Great Location Saves Millions in Dirt

We once worked on a project where the developer was choosing between two sites. Site A was five miles from existing infrastructure but had a lower asking price.

Site B was adjacent to existing utilities and roads but cost more per acre.

When we ran the residual analyses, Site B—despite its higher land cost—had a significantly higher residual value. The infrastructure savings more than offset the land premium. The developer bought Site B and saved nearly $4 million in backbone costs.

FAVORABLE ZONING AND ENTITLEMENTS

Zoning and entitlements are critical drivers of value. Higher densities typically mean more units to sell, which increases GDV. But density isn't everything—higher densities can also mean higher infrastructure demands for water, sewer, roads, and utilities, leading to incrementally higher infrastructure costs. The trade-off between higher revenue and incrementally higher infrastructure costs has to be understood and documented.

The ideal entitlement package includes not just density approval but also favorable development terms: locked-in fee schedules, approved financing mechanisms, flexible infrastructure phasing provisions, cost-sharing agreements, document oversizing requirements and payback mechanisms, and clear conditions of approval that don't require repeated trips back to the planning commission, city staff, and city council.

Jurisdictions willing to participate in infrastructure financing—using their funding (preferred) or through special districts, tax increment financing, fee credits, cost-sharing agreements, and/or reimbursement agreements—are particularly valuable. We'll discuss these tools in detail in the next chapter.

SPECIAL DISTRICTS

Special districts deserve special attention because they're one of the most powerful tools for engineering land value. These include but are not limited to: Community Facilities Districts (CFDs) in Arizona, California, Hawaii, and Washington; Community Development Districts (CDDs) in Florida; Metropolitan Districts (Metros) in Colorado; Public Improvement Districts (PIDs) in Texas and Utah; as well as Municipal Utility Districts (MUDs), Tax Increment Reinvestment Zones (TIRZs), and Municipal Management Districts (MMDs) in Texas.

The basic concept is the same across all these structures: providing timely, non-recourse, tax-exempt bond funding to construct public infrastructure or reimburse major public infrastructure improvement costs while shifting costs into an ongoing ad valorem property tax or assessment structure paid by future homeowners. Instead of the developer paying $10 million cash for infrastructure, a district issues bonds that are repaid by the homeowners through special assessments and/or additional ad valorem property taxes over 20 to 30 years.

This accomplishes two things. First, it reduces the developer's upfront capital requirements, freeing cash for other uses and reducing financing costs. Second, it shifts costs into the future, reducing project cash flow outflow velocity.

The catch is that the all-in special tax rates must be market-acceptable. Buyers won't pay premiums for homes with excessive property tax burdens. Sophisticated developers and their advisors (like Launch) carefully analyze tax rate tolerance to ensure special districts enhance rather than impair marketability.

Launch Tip: Think Like Both a Developer and a Lender

When evaluating projects, adopt dual perspectives. As a developer, ask: "How can I maximize returns?" As a lender, ask: "How could this go wrong? What would I need to see to be confident in this deal?"

The intersection of these perspectives is where good deals are made. A project that satisfies both the developer's return requirements and a lender's risk appetite is one that will be financed and built.

As a follow-up, I love what Charlie Munger says: "Invert, always invert. I sought good judgment mostly by collecting instances of bad judgment, then pondering ways to avoid such outcomes."

CHAPTER 5 PLAYBOOK: DIAGNOSING YOUR LEVERS

Chapter 5 ("What Impacts Land Residual Value?") explains the main drivers: cash flow, velocity, and discount rate. Now pinpoint where the real leverage is in your current deals.

Quick Actions You Can Take Now

1. *Identify the top three value drivers on a current project.*
   For one active project, ask:

   - Which assumptions (price, absorption, fees, infrastructure, financing) move the residual the most?

   - If you could only improve one of them, which would it be?

2. *Research fee credit, reimbursement, or various special district financing programs.*
   In the jurisdictions where you operate:

   - Are there fee credit mechanisms for oversizing or constructing public improvements?

   - Are special districts, reimbursement districts, or tax increment financing tools available?
   - Who controls access to those tools?

3. *Quantify the value of time on one deal.*
   Estimate your monthly carrying cost (interest, taxes, insurance, overhead) for a current project.

- Estimate the value of receiving your approvals six months earlier or the impact of a faster absorption period.

4. *Review your last development agreement with fresh eyes.*

Look at your most recent PADA or DA:

- Which protections did you secure on density, fees,timing,or special district financing?

- How did you address oversizing or funding infrastructure that benefits other landowners?

- Where are you still exposed to fee increases, policy changes, or delays?

How to Increase Land Residual Value—The Launch Approach

Now we get to the heart of this book: specific strategies for increasing land residual value. At Launch, we've developed a systematic approach to identifying and implementing value-creation opportunities. Everything we do is grounded in two principles:

- First, all value creation strategies must be based on proper planning and comprehensive documentation. Ideas don't create value; signed Agreements do.

- Second, the goal is to de-risk the transaction and then prove it on paper. Reduce uncertainty, then document what you've accomplished.

THE PROJECT VISION®

Everything we do at Launch starts with The Project Vision®: a clear picture of what the finished project will look like and how the developer will make money.

The Project Vision serves as the north star for all infrastructure and financing decisions. Every choice should move the project toward this vision. If a proposed entitlement strategy doesn't support the vision, it's probably not the right strategy.

Different business plans require different Project Visions®:

- **Plan-Entitle-Flip:** The developer plans to secure entitlements and sell to a builder. The Project Vision focuses on creating a marketable entitled asset.

- **Plan-Entitle-Develop:** The developer will take the project through horizontal development, creating super pads or finished lots for sale. The Project Vision must account for all horizontal costs and timing.

- **Vertical Development:** The developer will build and sell homes. The Project Vision extends through final home sales.

Here's a critical insight: even if you plan to flip the property after entitlement, you should still think through the full development process. Why? Because your buyer will. They'll evaluate the opportunity based on what they can do with it. If you've thought through the downstream economics and set up the project for success, your land is worth more.

THE PROJECT DANGERS, OPPORTUNITIES, AND STRENGTHS

Before developing value-creation strategies, we diagnose the project using the D.O.S. framework I introduced in Chapter 1. Let me go deeper into each component.

DANGERS

Every project has dangers—risks that could derail the project or impair returns. Smart developers identify these early and develop mitigation strategies.

Common dangers include:

- **Complex or Lengthy Jurisdictional Approvals:** Some jurisdictions require years of study, hearings, and negotiation before approvals are granted. (This is especially true in California, where a five-year entitlement process is considered fast.) Each trip back to the planning commission or city council is an opportunity for delay, modification, or denial.

- **Restrictive Zoning:** Zoning that limits flexibility can become a danger if market conditions change. What if the approved product type falls out of favor? Can you adapt?

- **Environmental Opposition and NIMBYism:** Environmental and/or community opposition can delay or kill projects.

Environmental groups, neighborhood associations, and "Not In My Back Yard" activists are formidable opponents.

- **Massive Upfront Infrastructure Requirements:** Projects requiring significant infrastructure spending before any revenue creates cash flow challenges and risks, precluding many projects from ever achieving their estimated return metrics.

- **Multi-Agency Coordination:** Projects that cross jurisdictional boundaries or require approval from multiple agencies (city, county, water district, school district, etc.) face coordination challenges.

- **Uncertain Public Funding:** Projects dependent on public funding commitments face political risk.

- **Changing Market Conditions:** Long development timelines expose projects to market risk.

Let me share some real-world examples that illustrate these dangers.

The Newland Communities "Sierra" project, north of San Marcos and Escondido in San Diego County, received approval from the County Board of Supervisors after years of planning. Then opponents put the project to a public vote through Measure B. The referendum was defeated, overturning the approval. Years of work and millions of dollars in entitlement costs were lost to organized political opposition. This is entitlement and political risk in stark terms.

On the positive side, a PADA can lock in favorable terms and reduce political risk. I worked on a PADA for Pulte and Vanguard on a large master-planned community in Arizona. The PADA memorialized key terms, including special district financing provisions, before annexation. This gave the developers certainty and reduced risk related to the establishment of the CFD (which was completed after annexation), which showed up as enhanced land value.

OPPORTUNITIES

Opportunities are the flip side of dangers: factors that could enhance value if properly exploited.

- **Land Seller Cooperation:** A seller willing to participate in creative deal structures (joint ventures, earnout provisions, seller financing, cooperation with special district formation) creates opportunities for better project economics.

- **Location Advantages:** Natural amenities (lakes, views, topography), adjacency to infrastructure, and proximity to employment and retail that create value that can be captured through premium pricing.

- **Jurisdictional Cooperation:** Some jurisdictions actively support development and provide tools to help. Jurisdictions that allow rights to run with the land (so value transfers to future buyers) are particularly valuable.

STRENGTHS

Strengths are the capabilities that the developer and team bring to the project.

- **Development Experience:** A track record of successful projects builds credibility with jurisdictions, lenders, and buyers.

- **Jurisdictional Relationships:** Prior experience with a jurisdiction can smooth the entitlement process.

- **Team Quality:** Experienced engineers, planners, legal counsel, and financial consultants reduce execution risk.

- **Financial Strength:** Strong balance sheets and access to capital allow developers to pursue opportunities others can't.

- **Specialized Expertise:** Knowledge of special districts, infrastructure financing, DIF credits, reimbursement agreements, cost-sharing agreements, value engineering, market conditions, or specific product types creates competitive advantages.

TOOLS IN THE LAUNCH TOOLBOX

With the DOS analysis complete, we turn to the strategies and tools available to enhance value. I organize these into four categories.

ZONING AND ENTITLEMENT STRATEGIES

Entitlements are the foundation of development value. Key strategies include:

- **PADA or DA:** Lock in infrastructure requirements, development and phasing conditions, density, density transfers, oversizing requirements (if any); DIF, permits/fees, etc., before final approvals. These provide certainty and protection against future policy changes.

- **Higher and Flexible Densities:** Negotiate entitlements that allow density optimization and flexibility to respond to changing market conditions.

- **Expedited Permitting:** Some jurisdictions offer fast-track processing for projects meeting certain criteria. Time saved is money saved.

- **Density Bonuses:** Many jurisdictions offer density bonuses for affordable housing, open space preservation, or other public benefits.

- **Pre-Approved Conditions:** Conditions that don't require frequent General Plan amendments or additional hearings reduce ongoing political risk.

SPECIAL DISTRICT STRATEGIES

Special districts are powerful tools for infrastructure financing. Key negotiation points include:

- **Bond Authorization and Types:** What types and amounts of bonds can the special district issue? What improvements are eligible for financing?

- **Maximum Effective Tax Rates:** What's the cap on special taxes and/or total effective property tax rates? This affects home sales marketability.

- **Value-to-Lien Requirements:** What ratio of fair market land value to bond principal amount is required? This affects bonding capacity and the timing of funds.

- **Governance Structure:** Who controls the governance of the district? Developer-controlled boards provide flexibility; public boards provide credibility but less control.

- **Selection of Professionals:** Who selects bond underwriters, consultants, and legal counsel? This affects costs and outcomes.

- **Assessment Methodologies:** How are costs allocated among properties? This affects fairness and marketability.

The concept we developed upfront finances future MUD infrastructure reimbursements using a conduit structure, bypassing certain jurisdictional constraints and accelerating cash flow into the project pro forma. This kind of creative structuring can significantly enhance project economics. This is just one of the innovative financing mechanisms we at Launch have created and implemented over our forty-plus-year professional history.

INFRASTRUCTURE COST MANAGEMENT

We use a framework called The RED Analysis™—Reduce, Eliminate, Defer—for infrastructure cost management:

- **Reduce:** Value engineer designs, negotiate better pricing, seek competitive bids, create special districts, determine DIF credits, negotiate cost-sharing agreements, establish reimbursement agreements, etc.

- **Eliminate:** Challenge whether all required infrastructure improvements are truly necessary. Sometimes requirements can be waived or modified.

- **Defer:** Push costs into the future where possible. Phase infrastructure to match absorption. Pay impact fees at occupancy rather than permit.

COORDINATION AND FUNDING SOLUTIONS

Complex projects often require multiple funding sources and coordination among stakeholders:

- **Special District(s):** Create special districts to fund construction and/or reimbursement of eligible public improvements out of bond proceeds.

- **Development Impact Fee Service Area Zones:** Establish DIF service area zones where impact fees from new development fund infrastructure that benefits the area. Note: The professionals at Launch are doing this more and more as the cost of public infrastructure continues to increase and the amount of funding from special districts is not fully adequate to fund all jurisdictionally requested public infrastructure.

- **Sales Tax Reimbursements:** Some jurisdictions share sales tax revenues with developers who create commercial development and/or fund large-scale public improvements.

- **Tax Increment Financing:** Capture the increase in property tax revenues from new development to fund infrastructure.

- **Reimbursement Districts:** Create mechanisms for early developers to be reimbursed by later developers who benefit from their infrastructure investments.

Launch Tip: How to Talk to Jurisdictions About Special Districts

Many jurisdictions are unfamiliar with special district financing or have misconceptions about it. When approaching jurisdictions, emphasize:

- *Special districts are a tool for financing infrastructure, not a way to avoid paying for it.*

- *The jurisdiction gains control over improvement standards and timing*

- *Future homeowners benefit from better infrastructure than cash-constrained development might provide*

- *Property taxes increase from successful development, benefiting all public services*

Position yourself as a partner helping the jurisdiction achieve its vision and goals, not an adversary trying to extract value.

Developer Beware: Political Risk Is Real (Sierra/Measure B)

The Sierra project's defeat at the ballot box is a sobering reminder that approvals can be reversed. Even after years of work and millions in investment, political opposition can derail a project. Mitigation strategies include building community support early, addressing legitimate concerns proactively, structuring Agreements to survive changes in political leadership, and maintaining realistic expectations about timeline and risk.

CHAPTER 6 ACTION PLAYBOOK: APPLYING PROJECT DOS™ AND PROJECT VISION®

Chapter 6 ("How to Increase Land Residual Value—The Launch Approach") introduces Launch's concepts of The Project Vision and Project DOS, and The Launch Sequence as systematic tools for engineering value.

Quick Actions You Can Take Now.

1. *Write a one-paragraph Project Vision for a key project.*
   For at least one property you control (or are targeting), answer:

   - What is the optimal end-state for this land?

   - Who is the ultimate buyer (builder, end user, institution)?

   - How does value get created and harvested over time?

2. *Run a quick Project DOS on a live or potential project.*
   On a single page, list:

   - **Dangers:** entitlement, political, market, infrastructure, capital risks

   - **Opportunities:** density upside, district financing,fee credits, repositioning

   - **Strengths:** team experience, relationships, location advantages, capital

3. *Compare your actual process to The Launch Sequence.*
   Take the stages described in Chapter 6 and ask:

   - Which stages do we execute well today?

   - Which stages do we rush, skip, or leave to chance?

   - Where would a more formal process likely add the most value?

Example of a Revised Land Residual Analysis

Now, let's put the strategies together and see how they impact land residual value. I'll present a before-and-after scenario showing how entitlements, special districts, and cost management can transform a project's economics.

Remember: all numbers in this example are illustrative. They don't represent any actual project, and they're designed to clearly show the impact of various strategies.

THE BASE CASE: BEFORE

Our hypothetical project is a 300-acre site with potential for 750 single-family lots. In the base case, we assume:

- No special district financing—all infrastructure costs paid by developer

- Full impact fees paid upfront at permit

- Conservative entitlements with no density flexibility

- Standard market pricing with no premium positioning

- No fee negotiations or credits

Exhibit 7.1 – Base Case Land Residual Analysis (Illustrative)

Description	Assumption	Amount
Revenue		
Home Sales	750 Homes / $550,000/Home	$412,500,000
Premiums	$0 / Lot	$0
Options/Upgrades	$33,000/Home	$24,750,000
Total Revenue		**$437,250,000**
Costs		
Home Construction Costs		
Direct Home Construction Costs	Avg. Home SF 2,225SF @ $67/PSF	$111,806,250
Options/Upgrades Costs	$21,200/Home	$15,900,000
Building Permit	$3,600/Home	$2,700,000
Soft & Financing Costs	15% (Costs)	$19,560,938
Builder Profit Margin	8% (Gross Revenue)	$34,980,000
Total Home Costs		**$184,947,188**
Finished Lot Value	Gross Revenue - Home Costs	$252,302,813
Finished Lot Value / Per Lot	**750 Lots**	**$336,404**
Site Improvements		
Backbone Infrastructure	$55,500 / Lot	$56,625,000
In-Tract Improvements	$95,350 / Lot	$71,512,500
Impact Fees	$25,400 / Lot	$19,050,000
Consultants	$5,500 / Lot	$4,125,000
Total Site Improvements		**$151,312,500**
Estimated Paper Lot Value	Finished Lot Value - Site Improvement Costs	$100,990,313
Estimated Paper Lot Value / Lot		**$134,654**
Land Residual Per Acre	**300 Acres**	**$336,634**

In the base case, the project generates a residual land value of about $101 million or approximately $336,600 per acre.

THE ENHANCED CASE: AFTER

Now let's apply the Launch approach. We'll assume the developer (working with Launch) has:

- Negotiated a DA with favorable terms

- Created a special district that will finance $32.8 million in backbone and on-site infrastructure through special district bonds

- Secured impact fee deferrals—fees paid at certificate of occupancy rather than permit

- Achieved a density increase to 775 lots through a density bonus for open space

- Positioned the project for 8 percent price premiums through amenity investments of $20,000 per lot

- Reduced certain soft and financing costs by 3 percent through streamlined permitting

Exhibit 7.2 – Enhanced Case Land Residual Analysis (Illustrative)

Description	Assumption	Amount
Revenue		
Home Sales	775 Homes / $594,000/Home	$460,350,000
Premiums	$6,600 / Lot	$5,115,000
Options/Upgrades	$33,000/Home	$25,575,000
Total Revenue		**$491,040,000**
Costs		
Home Construction Costs		
Direct Home Construction Costs	Avg. Home SF 2.225SF @ $67/PSF	$115,533,125
Options/Upgrades Costs	$21,200/Home	$16,430,000
Building Permit	$3,600/Home	$2,790,000
Soft & Financing Costs	12% (Costs)	$16,170,375
Builder Profit Margin	8% (Gross Revenue)	$39,283,200
Total Home Costs		**$190,206,700**
Finished Lot Value	Gross Revenue - Home Costs	$300,833,300
Finished Lot Value / Per Lot	**775 Lots**	**$388,172**
Site Improvements		
Backbone Infrastructure / Amenities	$75,500 / Lot	$58,512,500
In-Tract Improvements	$95,350 / Lot	$73,896,250
Impact Fees	$25,400 / Lot	$19,685,000
Impact Fee Credit	$12,750 / Lot	$9,881,250
Special District	Net Proceeds $42,350/Lot	($32,821,250)
Consultants	$5,500 / Lot	$4,262,500
Total Site Improvements		**$133,416,250**
Estimated Paper Lot Value	Finished Lot Value - Site Improvement Costs	$167,417,050
Estimated Paper Lot Value / Lot		**$223,223**
Land Residual Per Acre	**300 Acres**	**$558,057**

THE COMPARISON

The difference is dramatic:

Exhibit 7.3 – Before and After Residual Land Value Comparison (Illustrative)

Description	Base Case	Enhanced Case	Difference	% Difference
Gross Development Value	$437,250,000	$491,040,000	$53,790,000	12.3%
Total Home Costs	$184,947,188	$190,206,700	$5,259,513	2.8%
Estimated Finished Lot Value	$336,404	$388,172	$51,768	15.4%
Site Costs	$151,312,500	$133,416,250	($17,896,250)	-11.8%
Estimated Total Paper Lot Value	$100,990,313	$167,417,050	$66,426,738	65.8%
Estimated Paper Lot Value / Lot	$134,654	$223,223	$88,569	65.8%
Estimated Residual Value / Acre	$336,634	$558,057	$221,422	65.8%

The enhanced case shows a residual land value of over $69.4 million—more than 1.49 times the base case. The land value per acre jumps from $336,600 to over $558,100. Per paper lot, the value increases from $134,700 to $223,200.

WHAT DROVE THE IMPROVEMENT?

Let's break down where the value came from:

- **Revenue Increase:** More lots (+25) and higher prices (+8%) combined to increase GDV by $53.8 million.

- **Special District Infrastructure Offset (-$32.8M in costs):** The special district will issue bonds to finance $32.8 million in infrastructure, removing this cost from the developer's basis.

- **Impact Fee Deferral Savings:** Deferring impact fees to certificate of occupancy saves financing costs. *Note: Amount not estimated as a single column analysis performed. The financial impact would show* up *in the DCF.*

- **Reduced Soft & Financing Costs (-3 percent):** Streamlined permitting reduced professional fees, as did the lower cost of capital created by the special district financing.

Each of these improvements is the result of a specific strategy documented and memorialized in an executed and recorded legal agreement. The special district has been established with recorded formation documentation. The DA locks infrastructure requirements and impact fee timing. The density bonus is part of the entitlement approval. The price premiums are supported by a third-party market analysis showing comparable projects achieving similar premiums.

Launch Tip: Show Your Work. A Good Residual Analysis is a Sales Tool

When you're selling entitled land, the residual analysis isn't just for your internal use; it's a sales tool. Share your model with prospective buyers. Show them the assumptions. Provide the supporting documentation.

A buyer who can see exactly how the project works—and verify the assumptions—will pay more than one who's guessing. Transparency builds confidence, and confidence commands premium pricing.

The example above illustrates the power of comprehensive value engineering. A project was "upsized" through systematic application of the strategies we've discussed. In the chapters that follow, we'll dive deeper into cost control, market intelligence, and documentation—the keys to making these improvements real.

CHAPTER 7 PLAYBOOK:
TURNING "DEAD DEALS" INTO TRAINING GROUND

Chapter 7 ("Example of a Revised Land Residual Analysis") shows how dramatically a project can change when you pull the right levers. Use past and current project transactions as a training lab.

Quick Actions You Can Take Now

1. *Autopsy a project that didn't pencil.*
   Take a transaction you walked away from (or that failed feasibility):

   - Rebuild a simple residual with what you know now.

   - Find which levers (pricing, density, fees, districts,phasing) might have closed the gap, if any.

- Review your phasing and construction plans to determine what infrastructure could be reduced,eliminated, and/or deferred. Identify what special district you could have utilized to reduce improvement and financing costs.

- Consider other ways the transaction could have been structured, including: a joint venture structure, a lot banker, a phased land purchase, or seller financing.

2. *Quantify the impact fee burden on your next project.*
   For a current or upcoming deal:

   - Estimate the total impact/connection fee burden.

   - Ask, "What would a 25 percent reduction or credit be worth to the residual?"

   - Use that number to inform how much effort is justified in negotiation.

3. *Put a hard number on schedule risk.*
   Using your carrying cost estimate:

   - Calculate the dollar impact of a six-month delay vs. a six-month acceleration.

   - Use that figure when deciding how aggressively to pursue entitlement fast-tracking or phasing strategies.

Cost Control, Market Intelligence, and Financing Optimization

The land residual analysis identifies opportunities. Capturing those opportunities requires disciplined execution in three areas: cost control, market intelligence, and financing optimization.

COST CONTROL AND VALUE ENGINEERING

Value engineering is the systematic approach to proactively reducing costs without sacrificing the quality or marketability of the final product. It's not about cutting corners; it's about smart design, smart phasing, and smart decisions.

PRINCIPLES OF VALUE ENGINEERING

The fundamental question of value engineering is: Does this expenditure add commensurate value? If you're spending $100,000 on something that adds $150,000 in market value, that's a good investment. If you're spending $100,000 on something that adds $50,000 in value, you should look for alternatives.

Key value engineering strategies include:

- **Street Section Optimization:** Street widths, curb types, and pavement specifications significantly impact costs. Work with your engineer and the jurisdiction to optimize these while meeting safety and functionality requirements.

- **Utility Design:** Underground utilities are expensive. Optimize routing, sizing, and materials. Consider whether all utilities need to be underground or if overhead can be used in appropriate locations.

- **Grading Efficiency:** Earthwork is often the largest single cost category. Minimize cut-and-fill volumes. Export/import of dirt is expensive—strive for balanced sites.

- **Amenity Right-Sizing:** Amenities sell homes, but over-building amenities wastes money. Study what buyers actually value and design accordingly.

- **Phasing Strategy:** Build what you need when you need it. Over-building infrastructure for future phases ties up capital unnecessarily.

WORKING WITH YOUR TEAM

Value engineering is a team sport. Your civil engineer, land planner, builder, and consultants should all participate in value engineering sessions. Often, the best ideas come from people on the ground who see inefficiencies that aren't visible from the spreadsheet.

Schedule formal value engineering reviews at key milestones: after conceptual design, after preliminary engineering, and after detailed design. Each review is an opportunity to catch cost overruns before they're locked in.

MARKET INTELLIGENCE

Your revenue assumptions are only as good as your market intelligence. Garbage in, garbage out—if your price and pace assumptions are wrong, your residual analysis is meaningless. Additionally, if you're presenting overly optimistic and unsupported revenue assumptions to a buyer, you'll lose all credibility and open up every one of your assumptions to deep skepticism.

THIRD-PARTY MARKET STUDIES

For significant projects, commission independent market studies from firms like RCLCO, John Burns Real Estate Consulting, Zonda, the Concord Group, or Clarity. These firms specialize in analyzing housing markets and can provide:

- Market area demographics and trends

- Competitive supply analysis

- Price / Premium positioning and recommendations

- Absorption projections

- Product mix optimization

Third-party studies serve multiple purposes. They provide independent validation of your assumptions (or identify weaknesses you need to address). They build credibility with lenders and investors. And they often identify market dynamics that internal analysis misses.

ONGOING MARKET MONITORING

Markets change. What was true when you acquired the land may not be true when you're selling lots. Build ongoing market monitoring into your project management:

- Track competitive project sales weekly.

- Monitor price changes and incentive activity.

- Watch absorption rates across the market.

- Track economic indicators affecting housing demand (e.g., job creation, household formation, population, real income, mortgage rates, etc.).

Update your residual analysis periodically to reflect current market conditions. This keeps your financial projections realistic and identifies problems early.

Launch Tip: When to Spend on Third-Party Studies

Not every project justifies a $50,000 market study. But large projects, projects in unfamiliar markets, and projects with tight margins almost always benefit from independent analysis.

A good rule of thumb: if the land purchase exceeds $5 million, or if the project has more than 200 lots, invest in professional market intelligence. The cost is small relative to the value of better decisions.

FINANCING OPTIMIZATION

How you structure the acquisition and development financing significantly impacts project economics. The goal is to minimize upfront cash requirements while maintaining adequate capital for execution.

LAND ACQUISITION STRUCTURES

Consider alternatives to traditional cash purchases:

- **Options:** Secure control of land with an option payment while you complete due diligence and entitlement. Options reduce risk by limiting your exposure if the project doesn't work.

- **Phased Takedowns:** Purchase land in phases tied to development milestones or sales. This reduces capital requirements and aligns payments with cash generation.

- **Seller Participation:** Landowners may be willing to participate in the upside through joint ventures, earnout provisions, or seller financing. These structures reduce your cash requirement and share risk with the seller.

DEVELOPMENT FINANCING

For development financing, explore:

- **Traditional Bank Loans:** Secured by the land and improvements. Typically require significant equity and personal guarantees.

- **Private Lenders:** May offer more flexible terms and non-recourse financing, albeit at higher interest rates.

- **Institutional Joint Ventures:** Partners provide capital in exchange for a share of profits. Can reduce developer equity requirements, but it may come at a hefty cost.

- **Special District Bond Financing:** Through special districts, bonds can fund infrastructure without drawing on developer cash. This type of financing is non-recourse, tax-exempt (e.g., 4–7 percent) and passed on to homebuyers for repayment over 20–30 years. In essence, you, as the developer/builder, are borrowing money thatyou don't have to pay back, so long as your total effective tax rate is comparable to that of the other competitive projects. In every case where you can utilize a special district, we recommend that this financing mechanism be utilized as providing "turn-key" financing whose repayment is passed on to the end users will, by definition, enhance land value.

MINIMIZING CARRYING COSTS

Every day you hold undeveloped land, you're incurring carrying costs: property taxes, interest, insurance, and opportunity cost of tied-up capital. Strategies to minimize carrying costs include:

- Fast-track entitlement processes

- Parallel-path processing, where possible

- Phased development starting with revenue-generating parcels

- Pre-selling lots to builders before development completion

Developer Beware:
Cheap Dirt with Expensive Carry

I've seen developers attracted to "cheap" land that turns out to be incredibly expensive because of carrying costs. A five-year entitlement process at $500,000 per year in carrying costs adds $2.5 million to your effective land cost.

When evaluating land, model the full carrying cost through development. Sometimes the "expensive" land that's ready to develop is actually cheaper than the "cheap" land that requires years of entitlement work.

CHAPTER 8 ACTION PLAYBOOK:
MAKING COST, MARKET, AND CAPITAL WORK TOGETHER

Chapter 8 ("Cost Control, Market Intelligence, and Financing Optimization") is where many projects quietly succeed—or fail. Use these prompts to tighten your execution.

Quick Actions You Can Take Now

1. *Compare budget vs. actual on your last project.* Pull the final cost report and ask:

   - Where did actuals exceed budget by more than 10 percent?

- Were overruns driven by design scope, unit pricing,or unforeseen conditions?

- What could have been caught earlier with better value engineering?

2. *Build a simple competitive market dashboard.*
   For your primary submarket:

   - List at least five directly competing projects.

   - Track base prices, premiums, incentives, and monthly sales.

   - Update this monthly and feed the data back into your GDV assumptions.

3. *Estimate your weighted average cost of capital (WACC).*
   For a typical project:

   - Approximate the cost of each capital source (equity, bank debt, special district bonds, etc.).

   - Calculate a rough blended cost of capital rate.

   - Ask, "What would a 1 percent reduction in this blended cost be worth to my residual land value?"

4. *Inventory district financing options in your markets.*

For each state or region where you build:

- Identify which district tools (CFD, MUD, PID, CDD,TIRZ, etc.) are available.

- Note at a high-level which jurisdictions are open,cautious, or hostile to these tools.

- Flag at least one current or future project where special district financing could be feasibility-defining.

Partnership, Advocacy, and Memorializing Value

The strategies we've discussed only create value when they're successfully negotiated and documented. This chapter focuses on the "soft skills" of deal-making: negotiation, partnership building, and documentation.

YOU GET WHAT YOU NEGOTIATE

I've been in this business long enough to know that you don't get what you deserve; you get what you negotiate. Every favorable term in a development agreement, every reduction in an impact fee, every flexibility provision in an entitlement, all of these are the result of negotiation.

My philosophy on negotiation has evolved over the years. I've learned that:

- *Preparation is everything.* Know the facts, know the alternatives, know what the other side needs.

- *Look for win-win solutions.* The best deals leave both parties feeling they got a fair outcome.

- ***Be persistent but not annoying.*** Complex deals require multiple conversations. Stay engaged without burning bridges.

- ***Document everything.*** Agreements are meaningless unless they are in writing and are recorded.

That last point deserves emphasis. I've seen too many deals fall apart because someone assumed a verbal commitment or a written memorandum of understanding (MOU) would be honored. It usually isn't, not because people are dishonest, but because memories differ, circumstances change, and staff turnover. If it's not written down, approved, and recorded, it doesn't add value.

PARTNERSHIP AND ADVOCACY

Development is a collaborative process. You can't succeed by fighting with jurisdictions, agencies, and communities. You need partners.

WORKING WITH JURISDICTIONS

Approach jurisdictions as partners, not adversaries. Understand their goals: they want quality development, adequate infrastructure, a sustainable tax base, and community support. Show them how your project advances these goals.

Be a resource, not a burden. Come to meetings prepared. Provide complete financing plans and/or special district applications. Respond to staff requests promptly and thoroughly. Build a reputation as a professional who makes staff's jobs easier.

Engage early and often. Don't surprise planning staff with your special district applications. Meet them before you file. Understand their concerns and address them proactively.

WORKING WITH AGENCIES

Complex projects often require approvals from multiple agencies: state, county, municipal, water districts, school districts, transportation authorities, environmental agencies, and more. Each has its own priorities and processes.

Map the agency landscape early. Identify every agency with jurisdiction over your project. Understand their approval processes and timelines. Build relationships with key staff.

Coordinate approvals carefully. Agency approvals often have interdependence. You may not be able to get water approvals until you have environmental clearance, or transportation approvals until you have land use entitlements. Sequence your efforts to avoid bottlenecks.

WORKING WITH COMMUNITIES

Community support or opposition can make or break a project. The Sierra/Measure B example I mentioned earlier shows what happens when community opposition mobilizes.

Engage with communities early. Hold informational meetings. Listen to concerns. Address legitimate issues in your project design. Be transparent about what you're proposing.

Don't try to slip things through. Developers who try to minimize community engagement often face fierce opposition later. It's better to spend time building support upfront than to fight battles after the fact.

MEMORIALIZE EVERYTHING

I cannot emphasize this enough: Value is created through documentation. Every favorable term, every commitment, every Agreement must be memorialized in writing, and the writing must be clear, concise, understandable, and not subject to interpretation.

TYPES OF AGREEMENTS

Key documents that create and protect value include:

- **PADA:** Lock in development and financing terms before annexation to a city.

- **DA:** Comprehensive documents specifying development rights, use of special districts, alternative infrastructure payback mechanisms, impact fee schedules, infrastructure phasing requirements, and timing.

- **Special District Formation Documents:** For special districts, these specify bond authorization, tax rates, governance, and operational parameters.

- **Reimbursement Agreements:** Provide for recovery of infrastructure costs from future development or district revenues.

- **Cost Sharing Agreements:** Document the methodology for allocating infrastructure costs to other benefiting developers/builders, the party designated to construct the facilities, approving changes in scope and/or change orders, and how funding by the other benefitting parties will be provided, allowing costs of large regional infrastructure to be shared by multiple parties.

- **Impact Fee Credit Agreements:** Document the methodology of estimating impact fee credits for infrastructure provided by the developer and/or district.

These documents aren't just legal paperwork; they're the foundation of land value. When you sell entitled land, buyers will scrutinize these Agreements carefully to match the terms in the Agreements with the financial assumptions utilized in your land residual analysis. The quality of the terms in the Agreements and the comprehensiveness of your documentation directly affect the price you can command.

BUILDING THE PROJECT FILE

Think about the project file you'd want to see if you were the buyer. What would give you confidence that the value is real? That the entitlements will stick? That the financing mechanisms will work?

A good project file includes:

Entitlements, Land Use & Approvals

- Entitlement summary/approvals matrix (who approved what, when, conditions)General Plan designation and maps

- Specific Plan/Planned Community District/PAD documents

- Zoning ordinances and zoning verification letters

- Approved Master Plan/Site Plans/Land Use Plan (color exhibits + CAD where available)Conditions of Approval (COAs) from all agencies PADA and DADevelopment agreements (DA) with city/county

- Phasing plans and phasing conditions

- Recorded plats/tentative and final subdivision maps

- Variances and any deviations from code

- Annexation agreements (if applicable)School mitigation agreements/impact fee agreements

Ownership, Legal & Title

Current preliminary title report(s) and all underlying exception documents:

- Deeds and legal descriptions for all parcels

- Easements (access, utilities, drainage, open space, conservation, etc.)

- Encumbrances and restrictions (options, covenants, deed restrictions)

- Litigation, claims, or disputes related to property or entitlements

- Boundary surveys and ALTA surveys

- Cross-access/shared use agreements (e.g., with adjacent owners or commercial pads)

Environmental & Regulatory

- Phase I ESA; any Phase II ESAs and remediation reports

- Wetlands delineations and JD letters

- Biological reports (species surveys, habitat assessments)Cultural/archaeological reports

- Noise, air quality, and traffic impact studies

- NEPA/CEQA or equivalent documentation (EIR/EIS/FONSI, etc.)Environmental permits and approvals (404, 401, 1600, stormwater, etc.)

- Mitigation Monitoring & Reporting Program (MMRP) and status

- Hazardous materials reports (landfills, prior industrial uses)

Engineering, Infrastructure & Utilities

- Master engineering reports:

  - Water (supply, pressure, fire flow)

  - Sewer (capacity, routing)

  - Storm drainage/detention/water quality

  - Roadway and traffic/intersection improvements

- Approved construction plans (off-site and onsite):

  - Streets, grading, drainage, utilities

- Mass grading plans and earthwork balance studies

- Soils/geotechnical reports

- Floodplain and drainage studies (FEMA FIRMs, LOMR/LOMA if any)

- Utility commitment/will-serve letters (water, sewer, power, gas, telecom)

- Utility agreements, reimbursement, or oversizing agreements

- Status reports: percent of infrastructure complete by phase, punch lists, as-builts

Municipal, Districts & Public Finance

- Special District Agreements, Special District formation documents and maps

- Proof of passage of special district bond elections

- Special District Board Members Rate and Method of Apportionment (RMA) and current tax/assessment schedules (CA/HI/MA)Impact fee schedules and any bespoke fee agreements

- Reimbursement agreements (roads, utilities, regional facilities)Capital improvement cost estimates (by phase) and who pays what

- City/county staff reports and meeting minutes for key approvals

HOA / Master Association / Governance

- Draft or recorded CC&Rs (master and any sub-associations)

- Bylaws, Articles of Incorporation, governance structure

- Design guidelines/architectural controls/landscape standards

- Maintenance responsibility matrix (public vs HOA vs districts)Proposed or adopted HOA budgets, dues, and reserve studies

- Community rules and use restrictions (RV parking, rentals, etc.)

Land Planning, Product & Market

- Land use summary table (acres, units, product types, FAR, open space, etc.)

- Lotting studies and yield analysis by phase and product type

- Product program (lot sizes, intended home types, target price bands)

- Market/feasibility studies and absorption analyses

- Amenity plans and cost estimates (parks, trails, clubhouses, schools)

- School district information and school site agreements

Transaction, Economics & Business Plan

- Pro forma models:

  - Land Residual Model

- Historical cost-to-date detail:

  - Soft costs (entitlements, design, legal)

  - Hard costs (infrastructure, grading, utilities)

Operations, Compliance & Miscellaneous

- Service contracts (landscape, security, etc.)

- Insurance policies and claims history

- Ongoing regulatory reporting requirements (monitoring, annual reports)

- Access agreements, licenses, temporary construction easements

- Any prior marketing materials/branding (rights and restrictions)

Organized, professional documentation signals competence and reduces buyer due diligence timing and costs. Both of these translate to higher prices.

Case in Point: When a Signed Agreement Added Millions to the Price

A client approached us with a large landholding that had informal commitments from the city for favorable infrastructure financing. The land had been on the market with little serious interest.

We worked with the city to formalize the infrastructure financing commitments into a binding development agreement. Within three months of signing the develop-ment agreement, the property sold—for $4 million more than previous offers.

The difference? Certainty. Buyers couldn't rely on in-formal commitments. They could rely on signed Agree-ments.

Launch Tip: Build the Project File You'd Want Your Buyer to See

Before you go to market, review your project file criti-cally. Ask yourself: If I were buying this property, what questions would I have? What documentation would I want to see?

Then make sure your project data files answer those questions. Missing documents, incomplete and/or un-signed "draft" agreements, and unanswered questions cost you money—buyers discount for uncertainty, and they should.

CHAPTER 9 PLAYBOOK: PROTECTING ENGINEERED VALUE ON PAPER

Chapter 9 ("Partnership, Advocacy, and Memorializing Value") emphasizes that value isn't real until it is memorialized in binding agreements.

Quick Actions You Can Take Now

1. *Map your current holdings by Agreement strength.*
   For each major property you control:

   - Do you have a recorded PADA, DA, specific plan, or similar?

   - Or are you relying on general zoning, staff conversations, or policy "understandings" to support your assumptions?

2. *Draft a wish list of protections for properties without Agreements.*
   For one priority site without a strong agreement:

   - List the key terms you would want: locked-in density, fee caps, timing of payments, special tax district rights, reimbursement rights, vesting.

   - Use this as the starting brief for your land use attorney and negotiation team.

3. *Prepare a one-page "engineered value" summary.*
   For a current or upcoming project, create a lender or investor-ready summary that:

   - Shows baseline vs. "engineered" residual value

   - Identifies the key Agreements or districts that create that delta

   - Notes which of those are already executed vs. still in process

Pulling It All Together—Engineering Land Value

We've covered a lot of ground in this book. Let me pull it all together with a comprehensive framework and a composite case study.

THE ENGINEERING LAND VALUE FRAMEWORK

The process of engineering land value follows a logical sequence:

1. Understand Residual Land Value

Land value isn't what sellers want or what comparable properties sold for; it's what a developer can afford to pay while achieving required returns. The residual analysis is the tool for estimating this value.

2. Identify the Key Drivers

Three primary drivers determine residual value:

- Greater Margin (more revenues, less costs),

- Velocity (faster is better),

- Duration (more revenue sooner, and/or costs and expenditures later) and Discount Rate (less risk, lower the discount rate).

Every strategy works by moving one or more of these key drivers.

3. Diagnose with The Project DOS

Use the Dangers, Opportunities, Strengths framework to understand the specific factors affecting your project. Dangers must be mitigated or eliminated. Opportunities must be captured. Strengths must be leveraged.

4. Apply Multiple Entitlement, Development, and Financing Strategies

Deploy flexible entitlements, special district financing, infrastructure cost management, and creative funding solutions to improve project economics. Each improvement flows to the residual land value.

5. Document to Make Value Real

Memorialize all of the levers that move land value into binding Agreements with jurisdictions and agencies. Development agreements, district formation documents, fee credits, reimbursement provisions—these are the foundation of supportable/defensible, bankable land value.

6. Harvest Value

When the time is right, work with Launch and Land Advisors Organization to market the property to qualified buyers. A well-documented, fully entitled property with established infrastructure financing commands premium pricing.

COMPOSITE CASE STUDY: CANYON RIDGE

Let me illustrate this framework with a composite case study. "Canyon Ridge" represents a combination of projects we've worked on over the years—the details are illustrative, but the principles are real.

THE OPPORTUNITY

A family partnership owned 500 acres of ranch land on the edge of a growing metropolitan area. The property had good access, nice topography with some view lots, and was adjacent to a well-regarded school district. The family had received unsolicited offers ranging from $8,000 to $12,000 per acre, $4 million to $6 million total.

The family suspected the land was worth more but didn't know how to capture that value. They engaged Launch to help.

THE PROJECT DOS ANALYSIS

We started with a thorough DOS analysis:

Dangers:

- The property was in an unincorporated county with limited entitlement history.

- No municipal water or sewer service; it would require extension or on-site systems.

- Environmental groups had opposed other projects in the area.

- County staff were inexperienced with large-scale residential entitlements.

Opportunities:

- Adjacent city had expressed interest in annexation and was pro-growth.

- The city had an established special district program.

- Strong market demand—homes in the school district selling above regional averages.

- The landowner family was patient and willing to participate in the entitlement process.

Strengths:

- Launch team had prior experience with the city.

- Strong consultant team, including an experienced land use attorney.

- Family had resources to fund pre-development costs.

STRATEGY DEVELOPMENT

Based on The Project DOS analysis, we developed a comprehensive entitlement and financing strategy as follows:

- Pursue annexation to the adjacent city rather than county entitlement.

- Negotiate a PADA locking in key terms.

- Form a special district for public infrastructure financing with developer-friendly terms.

- Seek density that balanced market absorption with infrastructure capacity.

- Address environmental concerns proactively through conservation easements.

- Engage community early with project information and design charrettes.

IMPLEMENTATION

Over 30 months, we implemented the strategy. The city council approved annexation and a PADA that specified:

- 750 single-family lots across 450 developable acres (500 gross acres)Locked-in impact fees at the then-current rates

- Special district bond authorization of $35 million for public infrastructure

- Maximum effective property tax rate of 1.8 percent of home price 50-acre conservation easement satisfying environmental requirements

We also prepared detailed engineering, completed an environmental review, and commissioned third-party market studies to support pricing and absorption assumptions.

RESULTS

The before-and-after comparison was dramatic.

Exhibit 10.1 – Canyon Ridge Before and After (Illustrative)

Description	Before Case (Raw Land)	After Case (Fully Entitled)
Entitlement Status	Untitled	Fully Entitled with PADA
Infrastructure Financing	None	$35M special district established with authorization
Estimate Lot / Homes	Unknown	750 Lots
Estimate Value Acre	$25k - $33K	$125K - $150K
Estimated Total Value	$12.5M - $16.5M	$62.5M - $75M

The property was marketed by Land Advisors Organization with assistance from Launch to national builders. After a competitive bidding process, it sold for $64.5 million—over 5 times the highest unsolicited offer the family had received for raw land.

KEY LESSONS

The Canyon Ridge case illustrates several key principles:

- Value is created through entitlement and documentation, not just market timing.

- Special district financing significantly enhances project economics.

- Proactive management of Dangers (environmental, political) prevents deal-killing surprises.

- Patient capital and professional execution generate returns that dwarf quick sales.

- Partnership between Launch (engineering land value) and Land Advisors (harvesting value) maximizes outcomes.

YOUR TAKEAWAY

My goal for this book was to give you a working understanding of land residual analysis and how to use it as a decision and negotiation tool. If you've read this far, you should now be able to:

- Understand how land residual value is estimated and what drives it.

- Identify opportunities to enhance value through entitlements, financing, and cost management.

- Evaluate whether strategies proposed by consultants or partners actually improve your bottom line.

- Recognize the importance of documentation in making value real and bankable.

- Approach land transactions with greater sophistication and confidence.

This isn't academic knowledge; it's practical wisdom earned through decades of deal-making. Use it well.

CHAPTER 10 PLAYBOOK:
APPLYING THE FULL FRAMEWORK TO YOUR PORTFOLIO

Chapter 10 ("Pulling It All Together—Engineering Land Value") shows what happens when you run the full framework on a real opportunity. Use it as a template for your own assets.

Quick Actions You Can Take Now

1. *Write a clear Project Vision paragraph for one of your projects.*

   For the same property, write one paragraph describing:

   - The intended development program

   - The timeline in broad strokes

   - How and when land value will be engineered and harvested (sale of paper lots, finished lots, vertical,or some combination)

2. *Prepare a Project DOS for one existing landholding.*
   Choose a meaningful property (owned or targeted)and list:

   - Five **Dangers** that could impair value

- Five **Opportunities** to enhance value

- Three **Strengths** you or your partners bring to this site

3. *Estimate a baseline and an engineered residual.*

- First, run a conservative "as-is" residual using current entitlements, fees, and no district financing.

- Then sketch an "engineered" case that assumes:

  - Reasonable entitlement enhancements

  - Appropriate special district financing

  - Evaluation of reimbursement and/or cost-sharing agreements with other benefiting landowners

  - Realistic fee credits/deferrals

  - Identify the **three most important levers** that create the difference between the two cases.

Conclusion: An Invitation from Carter

If you've made it this far, thank you. I know I've asked a lot of you—this isn't light reading. But I hope you've found it valuable.

Let me close with a direct invitation.

If you own land, are looking to buy land, or are financing land development, and you want to enhance and harvest the value of that asset, I'd like to hear from you.

At Launch Development Finance Advisors, we help landowners, developers, and builders engineer land value through the strategies I've described in this book: entitlements, special district financing, infrastructure cost management, and comprehensive documentation. We're transaction-focused, which means we don't just produce reports—we help get deals done.

We work in strategic alignment with Land Advisors Organization, the nation's largest land brokerage firm focused exclusively on land. When it's time to sell, Land Advisors brings market knowledge, buyer relationships, and transaction execution that complements our value-creation work.

Here's what I suggest: Before you sell your land, before you commit to an acquisition, before you finalize your development plan, give me a call. Let's look at your opportunity through the land residual lens. We may find value you didn't know was there. We may identify risks you haven't considered. We may suggest strategies that transform a marginal project into an excellent one.

The initial conversation costs you nothing but time. If there's a fit and we can add value, we'll propose an engagement. If not, you'll at least walk away with some insights from someone who's spent over forty years thinking about these issues.

I got into this business because I love the puzzle of land development. Every project is different. Every project has its own challenges and opportunities. After all these years, I still get excited when we unlock value that others couldn't see.

I hope this book has given you some of that excitement—and more importantly, some practical tools to pursue your own opportunities.

Call me. Let's talk about your land.

Carter Froelich, CPA
Managing Principal
Launch Development Finance Advisors
Licensed Real Estate Advisor, Land Advisors Organization
C – 480-828-9555
E – Carter@launch-dfa.com
www.launch-dfa.com
www.thelaunchbond.com
www.launchlrs.com
www.landadvisors.com

Bonus: Role-Based Playbooks

Different participants in the land development ecosystem see the world through different lenses. The core principles of land residual analysis apply to all of them—but the questions each should ask are not the same.

Use this chapter as a quick reference based on various roles in the land value chain. If you wear more than one hat, work through each section.

For Landowners/Developers: Three Questions to Ask Your Broker or Consultants

"Have you run a land residual analysis for this site?"

If your advisory team is relying only on comparable sales, there is a real risk that you are leaving money on the table—or, just as dangerous, pricing the property above what the market can actually support.

"What tools—districts, fee credits, reimbursements—could apply here?"

The answer should be specific to your property and jurisdiction:

- Which district mechanisms are available?

- Are fee credits, reimbursements, or tax increment tools realistic?

- What would each tool mean for a buyer's residual?

"How would improved entitlements or financing change the buyer story?"

You may have the option before going to market to:

- Secure key entitlements

- Create or pre-entitle a special district

- Negotiate critical fee or reimbursement terms

Understanding how these steps change the buyer's pro forma helps you decide whether to invest in engineering value prior to sale.

For Developers/Builders: Three Changes to Make in Your Underwriting and Negotiations

Always include a residual analysis in your underwriting.

Don't rely solely on $/acre comps. Make a properly structured residual analysis the backbone of:

- Your internal investment committee materials

- Your negotiation position with sellers

Model developer/builder profit as an explicit line item.

Profit is not "whatever's left." Treat it as a required return for risk:

- Choose profit-on-cost, profit-on-revenue, or IRR as your metric.

- Make it explicit in your pro forma.

- Evaluate deals against that standard.

Separate wishful pricing from market-supported pricing.

If your pricing assumptions are more than ~10 percent above what the current, directly comparable product is achieving, you must have:

- Specific, tangible reasons (product, schools, amenities, effective property tax load)

- Third-party or market data backing those reasons

Otherwise, adjust your pricing back toward reality and rerun the residual.

Developer Beware

The most dangerous deals are the ones that pencil only because assumptions are aggressive. The discipline of the residual method is to expose every assumption to daylight—then decide if you truly believe it.

For Capital Providers: Three Questions for Your Investment Committee Memos

"What is the implied land residual at the proposed acquisition price?"

Have your team calculate:

- GDVAll-in development costs

- Required profit

- The resulting residual

If the proposed purchase price **exceeds** that residual, recognize that you are underwriting:

- Future price appreciation

- Cost savings that have not yet been achieved, or

- A lower profit requirement than is being stated

"Which entitlements and districts are assumed versus already papered?"

Insist on a clear distinction between:

- Approvals and agreements already executed and recorded

- Approvals and agreements the sponsor expects to obtain

Adjust:
- Required returns

- Leverage

- Covenants or conditions precedent

Based on how much of the business plan is still theoretical

"How sensitive are returns to timing of spend versus timing of revenue?"

Ask for sensitivity analyses on:

- Delayed approvals

- Slower absorption

- Changes in the phasing of major infrastructure spend

Many pro form as are more fragile to timing than to modest price or cost changes.

Role-Based Playbooks: Key Takeaways

- **Landowners** should insist that advisors think like value engineers, not just brokers of dirt.

- **Developers** should make residual analysis the center of their underwriting and negotiation strategy.

- **Capital providers** should use residual-based questions to stress-test assumptions and align risk with structure.

Quick Actions You Can Take Now

Identify your primary role right now.
Re-read the section above that best fits you (or read all three if you operate across roles).

Choose one change to implement on your very next deal.
Don't wait for the "perfect" project. Add at least one of the questions or practices from this chapter to the next transaction you touch.

Share this chapter with your team.

Use it as the agenda for a short working session:

- "What are we already doing well?"

- "Which questions or tools should we adopt immediately?"

- "Who owns implementing each change?"

Glossary of Key Terms

Absorption Rate
The pace at which homes or lots sell in a given market, typically expressed as units per month or per year.

Builder Profit
Builder profit is treated as a cost of production and represents the market price of construction services.

CFD (Community Facilities District)
An Arizona, California, or Hawaii special district that can levy special taxes (CA/HI) and/or special assessments, general obligation, and/or revenue bonds (AZ) to finance public infrastructure.

CDD (Community Development District)
Florida special district that can issue tax-exempt bonds and levy special assessments to finance infrastructure.

DCF (Discounted Cash Flow)
A valuation method that projects cash flows over time and discounts them to present value using an appropriate discount rate.

Developer Profit

The entrepreneurial reward for assembling land, securing entitlements, arranging financing, and managing risk.

Development Agreement

A contract between a developer and jurisdiction that specifies the terms of development, including permitted uses, density, fees, infrastructure requirements, and conditions.

DIF (Development Impact Fee)

Fees charged by jurisdictions to fund public infrastructure and services necessitated by new development.

GDV (Gross Development Value)

The total revenue expected from a development project upon completion—the sum of all sales proceeds.

Land Residual Value

The maximum price a developer can pay for land while still achieving the required return metrics, estimated by subtracting all development costs and required profit from GDV.

Metro (Metropolitan District)

A Colorado special district that can provide various services and finance public infrastructure through property taxes and fees.

MMD (Municipal Management District)

A Texas special district that can levy assessments and ad valorem taxes to fund public infrastructure and services.

MUD (Municipal Utility District)

A Texas special district that can issue bonds and levy taxes to finance water, sewer, and drainage utility infrastructure.

OPC (Opinion of Probable Cost)

An engineer's estimate of construction costs, typically prepared at various stages of design development.

PADA (Pre-Annexation Development Agreement)

An agreement between a developer and municipality that locks in development terms before formal annexation of the property.

PID (Public Improvement District)

A Texas special district that can levy assessments or a Utah special district that can levy special assessments and/or general obligation bonds to finance public improvements benefiting property within the district.

Project Vision®

Launch's term for the comprehensive business plan that guides development decisions, including the end-state vision and path to get there.

Residual Method

A valuation approach that determines land value by subtracting all development costs and required profit from projected revenues.

The D.O.S. Conversation® (Dangers, Opportunities, Strengths)
A diagnostic framework for evaluating development opportunities, adapted from Dan Sullivan's Strategic Coach methodology.

The Launch Sequence®
Launch's systematic methodology for identifying and implementing value-creation strategies in land development.

TIRZ (Tax Increment Reinvestment Zone)
A Texas financing mechanism that captures incremental property tax revenues from new development to fund infrastructure within the zone.

Value Engineering
The systematic process of reducing development costs without sacrificing quality or marketability, with the goal of enhancing land value.

About the Author

Carter Froelich, CPA, is the Managing Principal of Launch Development Finance Advisors, a transaction-based real estate consulting firm specializing in infrastructure financing, entitlement strategy, and land residual analysis.

With over four decades of experience in real estate finance and consulting, Carter has worked on hundreds of development projects across the United States. His expertise spans special district formation (CFDs, PIDs, Metros, CDDs, MUDs, TIRZs, and more), development agreements, impact fee analysis, and infrastructure funding strategies.

Carter began his career at Kenneth Leventhal & Company, one of the nation's premier real estate consulting firms, where he developed his foundational understanding of land valuation and development finance. He is a Certified Public Accountant and a licensed real estate advisor with Land Advisors Organization.

Carter is the author of *Land to Lots* and the *Bigger Future Land to Lots* trilogy, a comprehensive treatment of The Launch Sequence® methodology for engineering land value. He is a frequent speaker at industry conferences and a trusted advisor to landowners, developers, homebuilders, and capital providers nationwide.

He lives in the Southwest with his family and maintains an unhealthy obsession with the economics of dirt.

About Launch Development Finance Advisors

Launch Development Finance Advisors is a transaction-based real estate consulting firm dedicated to helping landowners, developers, and homebuilders finance infrastructure, reduce costs, mitigate risk, and enhance project profitability.

Our mission is simple: we want to be the hero to the development community. We accomplish this by financing infrastructure, reducing costs, and mitigating risks with the goal of enhancing project profitability and returns by bringing specialized expertise in:

- Special District Formation and Financing: CFDs, PIDs, Metros, CDDs, MUDs, TIRZs, MMDs, and other "alphabet soup" financing structures

- Entitlement Strategy: PADA or DA, density optimization, and jurisdictional navigation

- Land Residual Analysis: Comprehensive financial modeling to identify value-creation opportunities

- Infrastructure Cost Management: Value engineering, fee negotiation, and cost recovery strategies.

- Transaction Support: Due diligence, project structuring, and documentation for land acquisitions and sales

We work across the United States, with particular depth in the high-growth markets of Arizona, California, Colorado, Florida, Idaho, New Mexico, North Carolina, Tennessee, Texas, and Utah. Our team combines financial expertise, jurisdictional knowledge, and practical deal-making experience.

Unlike traditional consulting firms that produce reports and disappear, Launch is transaction-focused. We succeed when our clients succeed—when deals get done, when projects get built, when value gets harvested.

For more information, visit Launch Development Finance Advisors at Launch-dfa.com or contact Carter at carter@launch-dfa.com.

About Land Advisors Organization

Land Advisors Organization is the nation's largest land brokerage firm focused exclusively on land. With offices across the United States, Land Advisors represents landowners, developers, and builders in the acquisition and disposition of residential, commercial, and mixed-use land.

Land Advisors brings unmatched market knowledge, buyer relationships, and transaction execution capability to every engagement. Their agents specialize in land—they understand entitlements, infrastructure, development economics, and builder requirements in ways that generalist brokers cannot match.

Launch Development Finance Advisors operates in strategic alignment with Land Advisors Organization. This partnership allows us to serve clients across the full value cycle:

- Launch *engineers value* through entitlements, financing strategies, and risk mitigation

- Land Advisors *harvests value* by connecting sellers with qualified buyers

When you work with both organizations, you get a seamless path from raw land to maximized returns. We encourage landowners and developers to engage Launch early in the value-creation process and Land Advisors when the time comes to transact.

Learn more at LandAdvisors.com.

ENJOY A
COMPLIMENTARY
1-HOUR CONSULTING
SESSION

Meet one-on-one with Carter Froelich
to discuss financing opportunities
related to your development project.

SCHEDULE TODAY AT:
CARTERFROELICH.COM
Note: Projects should be 250 acres or more.

PODCAST

Carter Froelich hosts the *Land to Lots®* podcast where he and his team help their clients finance infrastructure, reduce costs and mitigate risks all with the goal of enhancing project profitability.

LANDTOLOTS.COM

LAUNCH®
DEVELOPMENT FINANCE ADVISORS